SHANTERA L. CHATMA

I0058005

emPOWHering

YOU:

12 TIPS FOR
FINDING
YOUR VOICE

emPowHering YOU

Copyright © 2018 by Shantera Chatman

This document is geared towards providing exact and reliable information in regards to the topic and issue covered. The publication is sold with the idea that the publisher is not required to render accounting, officially permitted, or otherwise, qualified services. If advice is necessary, legal or professional, a practiced individual in the profession should be ordered.

From a Declaration of Principles which was accepted and approved equally by a Committee of the American Bar Association and a Committee of Publishers and Associations.

In no way is it legal to reproduce, duplicate, or transmit any part of this document in either electronic means or in printed format. Recording of this publication is strictly prohibited and any storage of this document is not allowed unless with written permission from the publisher. All rights reserved.
The information provided herein is stated to be truthful and consistent, in that any liability, in terms of inattention or otherwise, by any usage or abuse of any policies, processes, or directions contained within is the solitary and utter responsibility of the recipient reader. Under no circumstances will any legal responsibility or blame be held against the publisher for any reparation, damages, or monetary loss due to the information herein, either directly or indirectly.
Respective authors own all copyrights not held by the publisher.
The trademarks that are used are without any consent, and the publication of the trademark is without permission or backing by the trademark owner. All trademarks and brands within this book are for clarifying purposes only and are the owned by the owners themselves, not affiliated with this document.
ISBN: 978-1-943409-59-4
All Rights Reserved

PTP
Pure Thoughts Publishing LLC
Printed in the United Sated of America

emPowHering YOU

Table of Contents

emPowHering YOU: 12 Tips for Finding Your Voice

"Never be bullied into silence. Never allow yourself to be made a victim. Accept no one's definition of your life but define yourself."
— Harvey Fierstein

emPowHering YOU

This book is not intended to be some profound piece of literature that tells a story of a young girl growing into a woman. This book is about practicality. One question I am often asked is what the most important component to women's empowerment is. In my opinion, the most important piece to empowerment is your voice. Without it, you are not complete. The journey to finding your voice is unique to each woman and her experiences. How I found my voice is very different from the way you have or will find your voice.

emPowHering You is intended to give you tips to home in on your voice and begin to explore what it takes to refine it. The book is designed to be read and worked through during a year. With monthly assignments, you will be able to ask yourself key questions and reflect on life experiences that have made you who you are.

So, let's begin.

"A girl should be two things: who and what she wants."
— Coco Chanel

emPowHering YOU

Tip 1: Define YOU

Before you can begin to identify your voice, you must understand who you are. Not who your friends, parents, or colleagues want you to be, but who you say you are. Often, we are so consumed by being who others think we should be that we lose ourselves. If that is you, we have some work to do before we work on your voice. Understanding who you are is one of the first steps to defining your voice.

Be mindful about what you are thinking and observe your patterns of thought. For instance, you might realize that you tend to feel that people don't care what you think and are not truly listening when you speak. When you start paying attention to your thought processes and patterns, you'll need to master what is called attentive non-judgment. This means being aware of your thought patterns and acknowledging them, but not beating yourself up over them. It is normal to have negative thought patterns. If you are aware of them, you can eliminate them from your mind. Once you start paying attention to the way you think about yourself and about the world, look specifically for the ways in which you identify yourself. What groups do you use to create your identity? For example, religion, nationality, sexual orientation, the roles you take on in your job, and even your role in personal relationships all play a part in how you define yourself.

So how should you define yourself?

Think of defining yourself like a 30-second pitch. In business, 30-second pitches are used to introduce yourself or your business in an efficient manner. You want to do the same to introduce yourself in other areas of your life.

With your 30-second pitch, you want to answer two questions:

1. Who are you?
2. Why should I care about you?

It may seem harsh, but no one cares who you are at first. You must make them care by defining yourself clearly and honestly.

I AM Times 5
Simply list five things that are true about yourself.
These can be statements like "I am loyal," or "I am a
thrill seeker." Whatever feels right for you.

1. _____

_____

2. _____

_____

3. _____

_____

4. _____

_____

5. _____

_____

emPowHering YOU

After reviewing the list, ask yourself if your items are gender-specific. If so, does it matter? Why or why not?

Monthly Assignment

Write your 30-second Speech. Be sure you align it with your I AM statements and practice it. Say it out loud and begin to embody the words. Begin to use it when speaking to others and take note of their response to you.

_____

_____

_____

_____

_____

_____

_____

_____

emPowHering YOU

_____

_____

_____

_____

_____

_____

_____

_____

_____

_____

_____

_____

_____

"Good fences make good neighbors."
-Robert Frost

Tip 2: Set Your Boundaries

What is a boundary? Simply put, a boundary is a limit or space between you and the other person; a clear place where you begin, and the other person ends. Scholars think of Robert Frost's quote and describe boundaries as a fence in your backyard. You get to decide who you let in and who you keep out, who you let into the whole back yard, or who you let just inside the gate. You may still be keeping a distance, but you are giving them a chance to prove their trustworthiness, both physically and emotionally. The purpose of setting a healthy boundary is to protect and take good care of you. It's all about YOU.

Boundaries help you to:

- **Define Your Identity** – you become clear and confident with yourself, and others know what to expect from you.
- **Protect Yourself from Violators** – boundaries let in what is good and keep out what is bad, so you remain safe and able to express your true self.
- **Bring Order** – without them, you are unable to regulate demands, ideas, dreams, responsibilities,

opportunities, pleasures and activities. Life can become chaotic.

- **Promote You** – leaders and employers with good boundaries know that if you have good boundaries, you can be trusted to state clearly what you can and cannot do, welcome input, and work passionately without burnout.
- **Protect Yourself from the Control of Others** – having clear boundaries makes it difficult for others to control you and makes it easier for you to say no when you need to.
- **Preserve Your Purpose and Mission** – once these are identified, boundaries save you for the relationships and opportunities that best fit who you are.

emPowHering YOU

5 Steps to Setting Better Boundaries

1. NO boundaries = low self esteem
Your boundaries are your values. Boundaries are representative of how much or little you respect yourself. Boundaries are your friend.

2. Decide What Your Core Values Are
Who are you? What do you value? Figure out what, exactly, you're comfortable with, and what you aren't. Once you get clear on what matters most to you, then you can take the bigger step of communicating this to others.

3. Decide Consequences Ahead of Time
So, what do you do if anyone pushes your boundaries (because they will)? Decide what the consequences are. The best way to figure out your own boundaries, and the consequences when people cross them, is to sit quietly down with yourself and make this all about you. (Remember: boundaries are about honoring your needs, not about judging other people's choices.)

4. Let Your Behavior, Not Your Words, Speak for You
Present your boundaries clearly to people, and then let your behavior do the talking. People WILL test,

push, and disrespect your limits. You'll know you're getting healthier when this doesn't get an emotional reaction out of you. When your boundaries are your core beliefs, you will not get riled up if you are tested.

5. Say What You Mean, Mean What You Say

The biggest part of boundaries is HOW CLEARLY you communicate them. You can have the healthiest set of boundaries on the planet; but if you do not communicate them clearly, you are going to create some confusing relationships, both for you and for everyone else involved. One of the quickest ways to get someone to question your character or authenticity: say one thing and do another. Sometimes we're afraid to confront others with truth in love or relationships. We're afraid to tell people what we really want. We conceal our true feelings because we're scared of people's reactions. The more you ground yourself with your boundaries and values, the more you'll be able to be very clear in your communication!

emPowHering YOU

Boundary Belief Assessment

Before you can begin to set new and improved boundaries, you need to look at what your existing beliefs about boundaries are. Your boundaries are built on the level of respect you have for yourself.

Select <u>one</u> answer for each boundary to gain awareness for how much you treasure yourself.

Boundary	Definitely True	Mostly True	Somewhat True	Not Very True	Hardly True, If at All
I have the power to make choices for myself.					
I am both valuable and imperfect.					
I am in a lifelong process of growth.					
My individual significance is not lowered or raised by others' opinions of me.					

emPowHering YOU

My life is enriched when living in interdependent relationships with cooperative and respectful people.					
My life is diminished when living in interdependent relationships with uncooperative and disrespectful people.					
My intrinsic, or built-in, value is neither more nor less than others'.					
Others' talents are a pleasure to observe and applaud.					
I value, like, and operate from a sense of gratitude, not entitlement.					
I can face					

challenges and meet problems.					
I accept and befriend myself.					
I believe I contribute significantly to the good of others and the world.					
It is my right and privilege to own my feelings.					
Boundaries are necessary and appropriate.					
Boundaries do not violate love.					
Setting limits is necessary to keep relationships healthy and vital.					
I am not compelled to justify a boundary with apologetic explanations.					

Monthly Assignment

Assess your Boundary Belief Assessment and concentrate on any boundary that is not marked as **Definitely True**. Ask yourself the following questions for each:

1. How was this boundary violated?
2. What specifically can be done to enforce this boundary?
3. What is the deadline for getting this boundary to **Definitely True**?

"Life is all about finding people who are your kind of crazy."

Tip 3: Identify Your Tribe

A tribe is defined as *"a social division in a traditional society consisting of families or communities linked by social, economic, religious, or blood ties, with a common culture and dialect, typically having a recognized leader."* In short, it's your group of people.

Here are a few reasons why it's important to find your tribe:

Accountability
Having a tribe means having people who know what your goals are and whether you're meeting them. Accountability is a sense of responsibility. While in the end you're only accountable to yourself, it's the perception of responsibility that makes having a tribe so important.

Knowledge
Everyone has special knowledge about something and having a tribe with similar interests can help you find the answers you need to meet your goals. Finding your tribe can help you become aware of things that you previously did not know about or

misunderstood. Through communication, you'll get the opportunity to broaden your own knowledge base so that you can help a tribe member in the future.

Support

Having a group of people who know you and wish to understand your struggle can be extremely comforting. Often, injuries and life events cause setbacks in training progress. A tribe of caring individuals can help you get through the tough stuff and get you back on track when you're ready to do so. Knowing you have a network of people with whom to celebrate your successes can be equally comforting. Having a tribe that shares your passion can add positivity and celebration, boosting your mood and helping you get started toward your next goal.

Motivation

The accountability, knowledge, and support you get from having a tribe all add up to one thing: motivation. Your tribe is the group of people who make you want to do more and do it better.

emPowHering YOU

Ways to Identify Your Tribe

1. **They show up**. Your tribe will come at any sign of need and will not require something in return.

2. **They allow you to talk about you**. Many so-called "friends" talk about themselves endlessly. And when you are talking they find a way to steer the conversation back to themselves. Your tribe doesn't do that.

3. **They love you unconditionally**. Your tribe sees you at your best and worst. They don't care if you make stupid choices in your personal life or get a bad haircut. They are proud of you and love you without condition.

4. **They are not judgmental**. If you feel exhausted after spending time with a "friend" because you are constantly defending yourself and your life choices, they are not a member of your tribe. Move along.

5. **They offer you random acts of love.** Texts of support, gestures on special days, and words of affirmation are acts of love.

6. **They are never in competition with you**. These folks celebrate your success as if it's their own. In a tribe, it's a feeling of "wholeness." Your joy is their joy.

emPowHering YOU

Monthly Assignment

Take an inventory of those that you call your "friends" and observe their actions based on the 6 Ways to Identify Your Tribe. Ask yourself the following questions:

1. Are you more concerned with the number of friends you have vs. the quality of their friendship?
2. Should s/he be a member of your tribe? If not, are you willing to remove them from your friend list?
3. Are you willing to have uncomfortable conversations with any "friend" that is not living up to your tribe expectations to save the relationship?

*"People won't have time for you if you are always
angry or complaining"
-Stephen Hawking*

Tip 4: Identify What Angers You

Feelings of anger arise due to how we interpret and react to certain situations. Everyone has their own triggers for what makes them angry, but some common ones include situations in which we feel:

- threatened or attacked
- frustrated or powerless
- like we're being invalidated or treated unfairly
- like people are not respecting our feelings or possessions

Whether your anger is about something that happened in the past or something that's going on right now, thinking about how and why we interpret and react to situations can help us learn how to cope with our emotions better. If you've experienced particular situations in the past that made you feel angry, such as abuse, trauma or bullying (either as a child or more recently as an adult), and you weren't able to safely express your anger at the time, you might still be coping with those angry feelings now. This might mean that you now find certain situations particularly challenging and more likely to make you angry. Conversely, if you're dealing with a lot of other problems in your life right now, you might find yourself feeling angry more easily than usual or getting angry at unrelated things.

29

emPowHering YOU

If there's a situation that's making you feel angry, but you don't feel able to express your anger directly or resolve it, then you might find you express that anger at other times.

emPowHering YOU

3 Ways to Use Your Anger to Your Advantage

1. Use it to help you conquer your fears
Anger is just fear in disguise. It doesn't matter what it is - fear of the unknown, fear of failure, fear of feeling small - fear can lead a person down a very dark path. You must learn to address the situation head-on and accept responsibility for the outcome.

2. Use it to fuel your creativity
Anger, when properly focused, can be a very powerful motivator. It can help reinforce your resolve, help you to overcome obstacles, and build grit. The challenge is to transform your anger into something positive and creative.

3. Use it to rally others to your cause
Anger is a universal emotion, and as such can draw others to support your cause. It's important (for entrepreneurs in particular) to find ways to use your anger to your advantage. Whether it's conquering the fears that give way to rage, or channeling it into a creative endeavor, you can find ways to rob anger of its destructive power and transform it into a powerful ally.

If you struggle with keeping your temper under control, below are some tips you can use to tame your temper. After all, the key to being an empowered woman is to understand all aspects of who you are and how to maintain control in all situations.

1. Think before you speak

In the heat of the moment, it's easy to say something you'll later regret. Take a few moments to collect your thoughts before saying anything — and allow others involved in the situation to do the same.

2. Once you're calm, express your anger

As soon as you're thinking clearly, express your frustration in an assertive but non-confrontational way. State your concerns and needs clearly and directly, without hurting others or trying to control them.

3. Get some exercise

Physical activity can help reduce stress that can cause you to become angry. If you feel your anger escalating, go for a brisk walk or run, or spend some time doing other enjoyable physical activities.

4. Take a timeout

Timeouts aren't just for kids. Give yourself short breaks during times of the day that tend to be stressful. A few moments of quiet time might help you feel better prepared to handle what's ahead without getting irritated or angry.

5. Identify possible solutions

Instead of focusing on what made you mad, work on resolving the issue at hand.

6. Stick with "I" statements

To avoid criticizing or placing blame — which might only increase tension — use "I" statements to describe the problem. Be respectful and specific.

7. Don't hold a grudge

Forgiveness is a powerful tool. If you allow anger and other negative feelings to crowd out positive feelings, you might find yourself swallowed up by your own bitterness or sense of injustice. But if you can forgive someone who angered you, you might both learn from the situation and strengthen your relationship.

8. Use humor to release tension

Lightening up can help diffuse tension. Use humor to help you face what's making you angry and, possibly, any unrealistic expectations you have for how things should go. Avoid sarcasm, though — it can hurt feelings and make things worse.

9. Practice relaxation skills
When your temper flares, put relaxation skills to work. Practice deep-breathing exercises or repeat a calming word or phrase, such as "Calm down."

10.   Know when to seek help
Learning to control anger is a challenge for everyone at times. Seek help for anger issues if your anger seems out of control, causes you to do things you regret, or hurts those around you.

Monthly Assignment

Make a list of 5 things that anger you and how you handle the anger. Ask yourself the following questions:

- Is the issue worth getting angry over?
- What more can I do to ensure this issue does not anger me anymore?

1. _____

   _____

   _____

   _____

2. _____

   _____

   _____

   _____

3. _____

_____

_____

_____

4. _____

_____

_____

_____

5. _____

_____

_____

_____

Anger Management Approach

_____

_____

_____

_____

_____

_____

_____

"Do fewer things and do them well. Focus on the things only you can do. Do the important things which must be done now."
-Eric Barker

emPowHering YOU

Tip 5: Identify What You Do Well

We are often faced with trying to understand what we do well when making important decisions or planning for a major change (personal or professional). It can be difficult to see our own skills as skills. Perhaps we don't see them as skills, but rather just things we do. Therefore, it is worth spending some time to make a self-assessment to find out what you are good at. The suggestions below are to help you understand your strengths, as well as how others see you.

- **Ask for Feedback**
  Often the people who you spend a lot of time with have a more balanced view of you than you have of yourself. Ask your manager or colleagues what they think your strengths and weaknesses are. Ask them to be honest, to help you get a clearer picture of what others think that you are good at. Listen without judgment. Write down their thoughts so that you can compare feedback from others and explore it further in your own time.
- **Assess What You Love**
  Write a list of the things that you love and analyze the list to see if you can identify any patterns. This will give you an idea of what you

are good at, or at least (and perhaps more importantly) what you enjoy doing.

- **Try New Things**
  By trying new things and pushing yourself outside your comfort zone, you may uncover your hidden talents. Commit to trying something new on a regular basis.
- **Get a Mentor**
  A mentor will be able to give you guidance and help you tackle some tough challenges you may face, as they might have been through similar challenges themselves. They will be able to use their experiences to guide you.
- **Reflect on Your Previous Accomplishments**
  Take some time to reflect on what you have already achieved; it is difficult to learn without reflection. Write down things that you consider to be great achievements. If you can see a pattern or repetition in your achievements, you might be able to identify what you are good at.

By understanding what you are good at, you can understand yourself more. This can be incredibly beneficial for your personal and career development, and help you to make better decisions.

emPowHering YOU

Monthly Assignment

The Building Blocks of Self: Your VITALS

Psychology Today published a great article that discusses the building blocks of identifying yourself. The basics of their research is below:

The capital letters in "VITALS" form an acronym for the 6 building blocks of Self, or VITALS, for short. The letters stand for: Values; Interests; Temperament; Around-the-Clock; Life Mission and Goals; and Strengths/Skills.

V = Values

Values - such as helping others and being creative - are guides to decision-making and motivators for goals. Research shows that just thinking or writing about your values can make it more likely that you take healthy actions.

I = Interests

Interests include your passions, hobbies, and anything that draws your attention over a sustained period. The focused mental state of being interested in something makes life vivid and may reveal clues to your deepest passions.

T = Temperament

Temperament describes your inborn preferences. Do you restore your energy from being alone or from being with people? Are you a planner or go-with-the-flow type of person? Do you make decisions more based on feelings or thoughts and facts? Do you prefer details or Big Ideas? Knowing the answers to temperament questions like these could help you gravitate toward situations in which you could flourish.

A = Around-the-Clock Activities

The "around-the-clock" category refers to when you like to do things. Are you a morning person or a night person, for example? At what time of day does your energy peak? If you schedule activities when you are at your best, you are respecting your innate biology.

L = Life Mission & Meaningful Goals

Ask yourself the same question: "What have been the most meaningful events of your life?" You may discover clues to your hidden identity, to your career, and to life satisfaction.

S = Strengths

Strengths can include not only abilities, skills, and talents, but also character strengths such as loyalty, respect for others, love of learning, emotional intelligence, fairness, and more. Knowing your strengths is one of the foundations of self-confidence.

Over the next month, pay close attention to the building blocks of self. Take note of your observations.

"Hope is being able to see that there is light despite all of the darkness."
-Desmond Tutu

Tip 6: Understand What Gives You Hope

Do you often find yourself struggling to see any meaning or purpose in your day-to-day activities? Do you want to break out of bad habits, but can't find the desire to do so? Hope might seem like a vague word, with perhaps little to no relevance to your life. But insofar as it means seeing the possibilities inherent to your life, it might just be a necessary precursor for you to get out of any rut you might find yourself in. Below are some steps to get you on your way to seeing more possibilities in your everyday life and circumstances.

1. **Figure out how you want your life to look**. People often struggle to hope for a better tomorrow, because they don't know what it might look like. Before you can have hope, it might be necessary to first figure out what type of life you imagine as the most desirable. Take some time to consider your ideal life, and what it would include.

   Ask yourself: "If I could wake up tomorrow and have any life, what would it be like?" Think about as many details as possible. What would your house look like? What would your friends be like? What kind of activities would you participate in? You may find it helpful to write out your vision for

45

your life so that you can review it and revisit it from time to time.

2. **Compare your ideal vision to your present life circumstances.** After you figure out what kind of life you would like to have in an ideal world, compare that life to your present life circumstances. Doing so can help you to determine what areas of your life are already in line with your vision, or whether you are headed in the right direction.

   For example, if you envision yourself 40 pounds thinner, consider what you are doing right now to get you to that goal. Are you eating healthy foods? Controlling your portions? Exercising regularly? What do you need to move closer to your vision?
   As you reflect on your life, consider your current circumstances. Have any of the aspects of your ideal vision already been manifested in your life?

3. **Consider whether you have realistic or unrealistic expectations for your life**. To have hope, it is important to make sure that the vision you have for yourself is realistic. If your vision is not realistic, it may cause you to feel hopeless. Consider your vision for your life and try to determine if your vision is realistic. If not, you may need to make

some adjustments so that your vision is something that you can achieve. For example, imagine your vision is to be a millionaire, but you don't know what type of job you would want to get you there. In this case, you should consider starting with goals that are more relevant to your current life conditions.

4. **Set some goals for yourself**. Having goals to work towards is one of the best ways to have hope. After you have developed a vision for your life, take time to set some goals. Write your goals out and work hard to achieve them. To improve your chances of reaching your goals, make sure that the goals you set are **SMART** goals. This acronym stands for the following features:

Specific—the goal is targeted rather than broad and/or vague
Measurable—the goal can be quantified (measured with numbers)
Action Oriented—the goal is something that you can actively work towards and control
Realistic-the goal is something you can achieve with the resources available to you
Time Bound—the goal has a beginning and ending or a deadline that you will hold yourself to

emPowHering YOU

Monthly Assignment

Keep a gratitude diary. Every night think of three things you are grateful for and write them down. Doing this every day will help you to develop a more hopeful outlook and it can also help you to sleep better and enjoy better health.

"Let the Beauty of What You Love Be What You Do"
-Rumi

Tip 7: Identify What You Have Always Wanted to Do with Your Life

Nine times out of ten , most people are not doing what they have always wanted to do. Maybe you decided to take the easy road, or you tried once, and it failed. Unfortunately, not following your passions will likely lead to regret and resentment towards others. It's time you reevaluate your choices and figure out a way to pursue your dreams. Here's a step-by-step plan for pinpointing your passions—and four ways to help you start turning them into your career.

1. Remember What You Loved as a Child

Often, our truest passions emerge in childhood, only to be squelched by real life pressures. Think about what you loved long before you had to worry about your career. Getting back in touch with those instincts is an important step in finding your passion.

2. Eliminate Money from the Equation

If money were no object, what would you do? Would you travel? Spend all your time with your children? Would you start a charitable organization to help abused women? Of course, money can't be ignored, but don't let financial pressures dictate your choices. Your career should ultimately lead to financial security, but if financial security is the defining motivator, it's unlikely you'll end up doing what you love.

3. Identify your Hero
Of everyone you know, either personally or in your extended frame of reference, whose career would you most want to emulate? Reach out to her to learn more about how she got to where she is, or, if that's not possible, read everything you can about her career and life.

4. Think of What You Enjoy That You Also Do Well
After you've done these exercises, think about what you've learned. Focus on the things that you both enjoy and do well and write them down. Then narrow the list to the top three or four things. Keep it handy, review it often, and use it as your jumping-off point when you're plotting your next career move.

emPowHering YOU

Monthly Assignment

Do a self-assessment to get closer to your truth, and closer to becoming the person you were meant to be. Ask yourself these questions:

1. What makes you feel truly alive?

_____

_____

_____

_____

2. What classes did you enjoy while in school?

   What do you like learning about?

_____

_____

_____

_____

3. What jobs have you held that made you feel

   purposeful?

   _____

   _____

   _____

   _____

4. What activities do you participate in that make

   you lose track of time because you love doing

   them so much?

_____

_____

_____

_____

5. What do people frequently tell you you're good at?

_____

_____

_____

_____

6. What ideas are you most passionate about?

_____

_____

_____

_____

"It's Not Hard to Make Decisions When You Know What Your Values Are."
-Roy E. Disney

Tip 8: Identify the Change You Would Like to See in You & Be It

We cannot begin to talk about being the change without talking about Gandhi. He is the authority on changing the world. The 10 tips below will help you to understand the change you want to see as well as how to become that change.

1. Change Yourself

If you change yourself, you will change your world. If you change how you think, then you will change how you feel and the actions you take. The problem with changing your outer world without changing yourself is that you will still be you when you reach that change you have strived for. You will still have your flaws and bad habits. In this new situation you will still not find what you hoped for, since your mind still has a lot negative stuff. Since your ego loves to divide things, to find enemies and to create separation, it may start to try to create even more problems and conflicts in your life and world.

2. You are In Control

What you feel and how you react to something is always up to you. There may be a "normal" or a common way to react to different things. But you can choose your own thoughts, reactions, and emotions to everything. As you realize that no-one outside of yourself can control how you feel, you can start to incorporate this thinking into your daily life and develop it as a thought habit.

3. Forgive and Let Go

Fighting evil with evil won't help anyone. Forgiving and letting go of the past will do you and the people in your world a great service. Spending your time in some negative memory won't help you after you have learned the lessons you can learn from that experience. If you don't forgive, then you let the past and another person control how you feel, which means you lose focus.

4. Take Action

To really get where you want to go and to really understand yourself and your world, you need to practice. Books can bring you knowledge. But you must act and translate that knowledge into results and understanding.

5. Be Present

The best way to overcome the inner resistance that often stops us from acting is to stay in the present as much as possible, and to be accepting. When you are in the present moment, you don't worry about the next moment. It becomes easier both to act and to keep your focus on this moment, and therefore perform better.

6. Understand Everyone Is Human

When you start to make myths out of people – even though they may have produced extraordinary results – you run the risk of becoming disconnected from them. You can start to feel like you could never achieve similar things because they are so very different. It's important to keep in mind that everyone is just a human being no matter who they are. Remember that we are all human and prone to make mistakes. Holding people to unreasonable standards will only create more unnecessary conflicts in your world, and negativity within you. The problem with social media is people get to edit their lives prior to viewing. We are now living in one big reality show that never ends. Sometimes we must unplug to re-align with what is real. Allow yourself to see with clarity where you went wrong and what you can learn from your own mistakes.

7. Don't Quit

One reason Gandhi was so successful with his method of non-violence was because he and his followers were so persistent. They just didn't give up. Success or victory will seldom come as quickly as you would like it to. I think one of the reasons people don't get what they want is simply because they give up too soon. The time they think an achievement will require isn't the same amount of time it usually takes to achieve that goal.

8. See the Good in People and Help Them

When you see the good in people, it becomes easier to motivate yourself to be of service to them. By being of service to other people, by giving them value, you make their lives better. But that's merely the beginning. Over time you tend to get what you give. The people you help may feel more inclined to help other people. Together you will create an upward spiral of positive change that grows and becomes stronger.

9. Be You

When your words and thoughts are aligned, it shows in your communication. If your actions are in alignment with what you're communicating, then you start to create your own belief in what you can do. In turn, you will see others begin to believe in you too.

10.　　Continue to Grow

You may look inconsistent or like you don't know what you are doing from time to time. Don't let that discourage you. The road to consistency takes time and work. To choose to grow and evolve is a happier and more useful path to take.

emPowHering YOU

Monthly Assignment

The 10 areas discussed will require some time to implement. During this month, choose two areas that you would like to improve upon, and put a plan in place to move ahead. In the space below, outline your plan of action for each.

1. _____

_____

_____

_____

_____

_____

_____

_____

_____

_____

_____

_____

_____

2. _____

_____

_____

_____

_____

_____

_____

_____

"The word 'listen' contains the same letters as the word 'silent'."
— Alfred Brendel

Tip 9: Cultivate Your Ability to Listen

Have you ever been told, "You aren't listening to me!"? Have you found it more difficult to listen well as demands increase in your life and the pace quickens? The impact of distracted and unfocused listening is often problematic and damaging to productivity levels and relationships. Listening is one of, if not the most powerful, ways we communicate. Listening skills account for at least 75% of communication interactions, and are a key factor leading to success or derailment in business transactions. Whether or not someone feels truly heard and understood has a quantitative and qualitative impact on the clarity of communication, trust, defensiveness, and thus, personal and professional effectiveness. As we become more aware of and attentive to how we listen, the relationships in all areas of life begin to strengthen and become more collaborative.

✓ **Understand that most communication is non-verbal**
   Although it may seem counterintuitive, when we listen to others we are communicating something. The question is—what are we communicating? If we listen well, then we

communicate our care and concern for the other person. When we fail to genuinely listen, we communicate our lack of concern.

✓ Listen before you speak

Like breaking any other habit, it may take some time. Being a good listener is more than just having the right technique. It also involves being genuinely interested in what others have to say. Do you truly care about the opinions of others? If you want to become a good listener, start coaching yourself to listen before you speak. And give yourself some time to break old habits.

✓ Think of the person you know who listens best, and copy her

Try to think of someone who leans in when you speak, focuses intently on your every word, and always expresses the right kinds of emotions to match what you are communicating. If she doesn't understand, she asks for clarification. She puts down technology and makes you feel like you're the most important person in the world. If you know someone that fits that description, follow their lead.

Monthly Assignment

Are you an active listener? Do you often get calls from friends and colleagues asking you to listen to their problems? Over the next month, keep a log of the times you allowed someone to control the conversation and you remained silent. If you do not have at least **two instances** of active listening, you should review the tips in this chapter again and make a concerted effort to become a better listener.

<u>Listening Log</u>

Date	Conversation With

"Don't you ever let a soul in the world tell you that you can't be exactly who you are."
— Lady Gaga

Tip 10: Get Objective. See Yourself from Another POV

It's difficult to step outside ourselves and try to see ourselves as others see us. For example, let's say you're trying to create a certain outcome at work and in your mind (that is, your self-created reality) you see yourself as being a strong, powerful leader. Meanwhile those in your charge see you as being a self-important, power-tripping, egomaniac. How you are perceived matters.

In that example, you have a perception problem, an awareness problem, and a communication issue. Your staff are not 'getting' what you believe you're giving them. All too often, bosses see themselves as being strong, focused, and assertive while (a percentage of) the people around them see them as intimidating, insensitive, and unaware.

In any meaningful relationship – whether personal or professional – it is important that we have a level of insight into, and, understanding of, how people perceive us. Not so that we might stress, worry and become (more) insecure about what people think (we already do that too much), but rather so that we might develop more empowered, meaningful, productive, and enjoyable relationships. Greater connection. Better understanding. More effective communication.

We can only make real progress with people when we begin to understand their (version of) reality. We don't need to embrace it or agree with it, just understand it. And them.

So, should we get all weird, anxious, and paranoid about what people think of us? Of course not; that's a negative, not a positive, and totally not what this lesson is about. But what we should do is endeavor to become more aware and 'in tune' when it comes to the issue of how we're perceived by the people in our world. The greater our awareness of how others see us, the more effective we become (on a range of levels). The more effective we become, the more connection we create (which means better understanding), and the less relationship and communication problems we'll experience.

How do we become more aware of how people see us – again, not to be confused with obsessing (worrying) about what people think – to produce better results in our world? The answer is: consciously, intentionally, and un-emotionally. That last one is the tough bit. All the information is there, we just need to look for it and interpret it for what it is.

emPowHering YOU

People are constantly telling us what they think and how they feel via their actions, behaviors, choices, reactions, and body-language. The problem is we don't usually pay attention. We don't read the signs. We don't 'listen' to the non-verbal stuff, which is where most of the communication comes from. People's physiology (facial expressions, eye contact, posture, hand movements, respiration, and even perspiration levels) will usually tell us more than their words.

When we go into familiar situations and environments with a totally different perspective, it's amazing what we discover. You want to know what people really think? Pay attention.

Warning: Don't let your low self-esteem or propensity to find offense get in the way of the value in this message. Knowing how others see you or what they think of you should not come from a place of fear, insecurity or seeking approval, but rather from a desire to create better connection, understanding, and results in your world.

By taking another person's point of view, we broaden our own. In doing so, we become aware of not only our own actions, but the consequences of those actions. Understanding both action and consequence can lead us to ownership, and fortify our sense of personal responsibility, because it puts us in a place where nothing is assumed, and we are beholden to consider all sides of a situation.

The level of sensitivity and compassion that this perspective breeds is enormous. It moves us from ego-centricity to ethno-centricity - from "me" to "us" -- and that, in the best of all possible worlds, can then lead us to geo-centricity, or "all of us". Ultimately, this reveals our humanity and the true spirit of service with the imperative "my actions are here to serve you." In the end, we're here to help, not hinder, one another.

emPowHering YOU

Monthly Assignment

Understanding your impact on others is key to understanding how to broaden your perspective. Think of one or two trusted people in your inner circle. Ask them the key questions below and record their answers. Afterward, analyze your thoughts about who you are and your place in the world. Ask yourself this: How does the feedback change your point of view?

   1. How would you describe me in less than 5 words?

_____

_____

_____

_____

_____

_____

2. Do you consider me to be a good person/leader?

_____

_____

_____

_____

_____

_____

_____

"Honesty is the first chapter in the book of wisdom"
-Thomas Jefferson

Tip 11: Get Honest with Yourself

Being true to yourself is a life-long practice that requires commitment and re-commitment, moment to moment, as you grow and evolve. The answer to what is true for you always exists at the core of who you are, if you give yourself the space and time to listen. When you are being true to yourself, you are completely honest with what you feel, deeply value, and desire. It also means communicating your feelings wholeheartedly both with yourself and others, allowing your truth to flow through you and into the world.

To know your truth fully and express it authentically, you first need to cultivate a deep and trusting relationship with yourself. Ultimately, this begins with awareness of your thoughts, as well as awareness of your whole-body experience, and how you interact with the world each day. You can expand your awareness and strengthen the connection with yourself through introspective practices such as meditation, yoga, and journal writing. These practices help you become more present and establish reference points to identify when you are (or are not) living in alignment with the deeper aspect of yourself. The more you practice, the easier it becomes to self-correct when you are out of alignment.

Understanding when you are in alignment or out of alignment may often be based on an intuitive feeling rather than a thought. Feelings of openness, expansion, inner joy, and freedom are good signs that you are on the right path. Conversely, if you are not being true to yourself, it may show up through feelings of contraction and tension, unease, disconnection, resignation, emptiness, discontentment, or a lack of fulfillment. By learning to pay attention to your deeper senses and feelings, and by cultivating greater awareness in your life, you can establish a strong connection to yourself and feel confident in knowing what is deeply true for you. But what is true also yearns to be expressed. It is up to each of us to be courageous in bringing forth our own truth, expressing it fully and authentically in the world.

Let's discuss some of the reasons it's important to be honest with yourself:

- **You become mentally strong.**
  When you are connected to your core truth and values, you aren't affected by others'

negative opinions of you. You know who you are, and don't believe you need to change.

- **You know what you want.**
  If you build your identity on the fluctuating foundation of public opinion, nothing will be constant. To pursue what you want, you must be able to rely on yourself.

- **You can be honest with others.**
  No relationship can survive, let alone thrive, without honesty. And if you are hiding your truth from yourself, how will you ever find it to share it with someone else? Relationships that are healthy, happy, and balanced are comprised of people who are in touch with their authentic selves.

- **You have clarity.**
  Lies will always keep you stuck, and only hurt the person holding them. When you are honest with yourself, you will always know what you need to do, even if it's difficult.

- **You become more responsible for both your choices and their consequences.**
  Acceptance of responsibility is foundational to changing your life in a positive way. Changing

is not simply "changing," it is *evolving*. As you evolve, the world responds by offering you new opportunities to understand yourself.

Monthly Assignment

It is now time to do some digging. Ask yourself the following questions, and remember to think about each question clearly:

Why am I doing "X" behavior?

_____

_____

_____

_____

_____

_____

_____

_____

emPowHering YOU

What don't I want my best friend or spouse to know about me?

_____

_____

_____

_____

_____

_____

_____

What's my next step?

_____

_____

emPowHering YOU

"Always remember you are braver than you believe, stronger than you seem, and smarter than you think."
-Christopher Robin

Tip 12: Find Someone That Believes in You. (Hint: This Should Be YOU)

Karen David at Live Life Well says, "When someone believes in you, everything can change — fear decreases, confidence increases, the bravery to aim higher and take a leap grows". As we grow older and learn more about the world, doubt starts to creep in. Even though our parents stand behind us, we often self-impose limits, and compare ourselves to others. The days of fearless leaps may have come to an end. But what happens when others believe in you?

They highlight our best qualities. When someone is specific about why they believe in you, it can often make you more aware of and more confident in your strengths. If your girlfriends proclaim that you can organize people's chaos-ridden closets better than anyone, could it inspire you to go into business as a professional organizer? When people point out our talents, it helps us examine them, fine tune them, and use them more confidently in our lives.

They help us focus on the positive. Unfortunately, many of us are quick to focus more of our attention on our faults than on our strengths. When others believe in us, they note the positive and help us change our focus. Positivity is powerful.

They teach us to believe more in ourselves. When someone truly believes in you, that feeling becomes contagious. Hearing about your best qualities, focusing on the "cans" instead of "can'ts", and meeting or exceeding expectations changes the way you think and feel about yourself. Johann Wolfgang von Goethe said, "Magic is believing in yourself, and if you can do that, you can make anything happen."

emPowHering YOU

Monthly Assignment

Think about how others try to encourage you to do more. What do they say you are good at? How does that make you feel? Are you motivated to do more?

In which areas of your life have you been encouraged to do more?

1. _____

_____

_____

_____

2. _____

_____

_____

_____

_____

3. _____

_____

_____

_____

In what ways have you taken that encouragement and made changes in your life?

_____

_____

_____

_____

_____

emPowHering YOU

In Summation

I mentioned in the beginning of this book that its designed to have you work through the tips during the course of a year. Now that you have read all 12 tips, you should understand why a year is appropriate. Some of the activities require intense thought, and even some difficult conversations. These are not things that can be accomplished in a week. Understanding your boundaries or finding your tribe should not be taken lightly, and in some cases may take more than a month to solidify. If that is the case, take all the time you need. Do not rush it. The journey to who you are and identifying your voice is very important and should not be taken for granted.

It is not lost on me that the tips are not rocket science. The ideas are not unique, but the notion of using the tips in sequential order to develop a better understanding of who you are may be. The monthly activities simply take the narratives to the next step. It's one thing to read about making a change, it's another to begin to move forward toward that change.

My goal is to add value to anyone who reads this book and aid them in their journey. Our voices may differ based on political views, cultural backgrounds, and even education, but how we search, find, and understand that voice requires similar tasks. I hope you enjoy your journey to you, and I hope to hear from you along the way.

Shantera

About The Author

Shantera Chatman is a strategic organizational engagement and adoption consultant with experience in organizational change management (OCM), project management, process improvements and transition leadership. With almost 20 years of experience spanning the Aerospace and Oil & Gas Industries, she has a reputation for building strong relationships with her clients and delivering quality results.

While working as a consultant for the Johnson Space Center, Shantera founded the Annual Women's Empowerment

Conference (AWEC) in 2008 after volunteering for over a year at a local women's shelter. She later founded The Chatman Women's Foundation to provide scholarships and grants to women building businesses, going back to school or even getting out of shelters.

Shantera has worked for both large and small consulting firms servicing clients such as NASA, Chevron and BHP Billiton. For her clients, Shantera has led teams as they successfully roll out various IT and cyber intelligence initiatives. As an OCM specialist and project manager, Shantera has helped Fortune 500 companies engage their user community and adopt changes in the workplace. She approaches a problem with a "roll-up your sleeves" mentality and does not simply consult on a problem; she is instrumental in developing the solution.

Shantera is a sought after speaker that focuses on leadership, women's empowerment and people engagement. All of the skills acquired throughout her career make Shantera a strong leader in the community and any organization she chooses to engage.

emPowHering YOU

Shantera is the author of PowHer Play: A Women's Empowerment Guide and Embrace Resistance: How to Conquer Your Critics.

www.ingramcontent.com/pod-product-compliance
Lightning Source LLC
Chambersburg PA
CBHW020158200326
41521CB00006B/420